CONTENTS

MW00568244

Encouraging Interest

Help students to develop an understanding and appreciation for different artists and types of art by highlighting a variety of artists each month. Display examples of an artist's artwork and have students study and duplicate their style. In addition, encourage students to visit art museums online or visit local art galleries.

Student Sketchbook Ideas

Give each student a large sketchbook in which to explore art techniques, create designs, collect examples of artwork they admire and challenge their thinking about art. Encourage students to add to their sketchbook at least once a week.

Colouring Pages

These pages are intended to give students practice in using different elements of design.

Rubrics and Checklists

Use the rubrics in this book to assess student learning.

Learning Logs

In addition to a sketchbook have students keep a learning log as an effective way for students to organize their thoughts and ideas about art concepts presented. Learning logs can include the following kinds of entries:

- teacher journal prompts
- student personal reflections
- questions that arise
- connections discovered
- labelled diagrams

Art Glossary

List new art vocabulary and meanings on chart paper for students' reference during activities.

ELEMENTS OF DESIGN: COLOUR

Activity 1: Creating Mood

What you need:

• Colouring materials such as pencil crayons, pastels, watercolours or crayons • Paper

What to do:

1. Ask students if they think colour can create a mood, or strong feeling. Discuss how. Brainstorm ways that warm colours can affect mood and ways that cool colours can affect mood.

2. Have students create a picture or design with an overall mood. Themes that students can choose to illustrate include:
   • a fantasy world or creature
   • an underwater environment
   • a futuristic world

3. When they have completed their artwork, have students write a journal entry to explain the mood they were trying to create and how they chose and used colours to do it.

Activity 2: Complementary Colours

What you need:

• Paper
• Watercolours
• Paintbrushes
• Rulers
• Black markers
• Pencils

What to do:

1. Review with students the concept of complementary colours. These are colours that are directly opposite each other on the colour wheel. For example, red and green or blue and orange.

2. Next, tell students that they are going to create an abstract complementary painting.

3. Instruct students to produce a design of black outlines of overlapping abstract shapes. Encourage students to use spirals, diagonals and other types of lines.

4. Have students choose and use complementary colours to paint the sections of their design.

2

THE COLOUR WHEEL

The **colour wheel** is a colour circle based on red, yellow and blue.

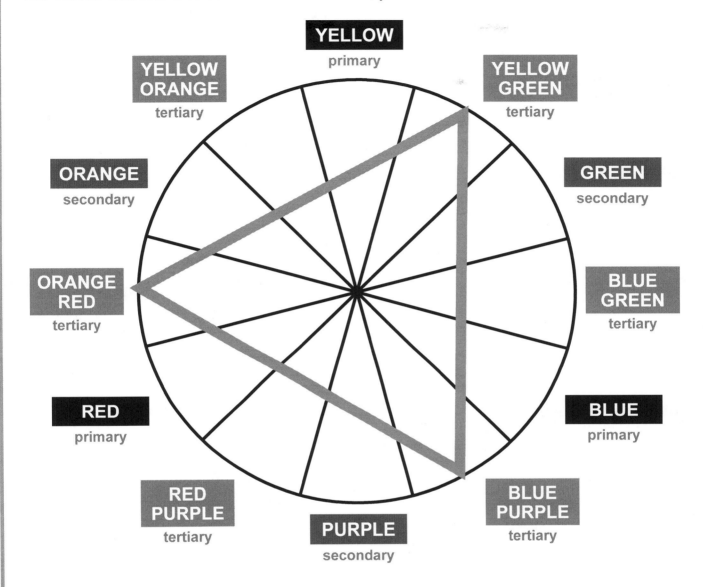

YELLOW — primary
YELLOW ORANGE — tertiary
YELLOW GREEN — tertiary
ORANGE — secondary
GREEN — secondary
ORANGE RED — tertiary
BLUE GREEN — tertiary
RED — primary
BLUE — primary
RED PURPLE — tertiary
PURPLE — secondary
BLUE PURPLE — tertiary

The **primary colours** are red, yellow and blue. Primary colours cannot be mixed or created by any combination of other colours.

The **secondary colours** are purple, green and orange. These colours are created by mixing the primary colours.

The **tertiary colours** are created by mixing a primary and a secondary colour.

Complementary colours are any two colours that are opposite each other on the colour wheel, such as red and green or blue and orange. In theory, opposite colours create maximum contrast.

The colour wheel is _____

_____

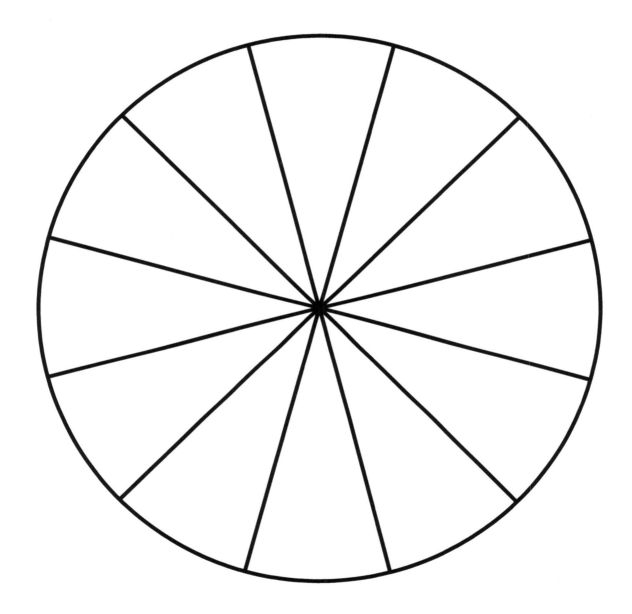

THE COLOUR WHEEL

Primary Colours

_____

_____

Secondary Colours

_____

_____

Tertiary Colours

_____

_____

_____

_____

Complementary Colours

_____

_____

_____

_____

CONTRASTING COLOURS

Contrast: A principle of design where light colours are used next to dark colours.

Test different colour combinations on another piece of paper. Then copy the combinations that best match the descriptions below.

STRONGEST CONTRAST

LEAST CONTRAST

FAVOURITE COMBINATIONS

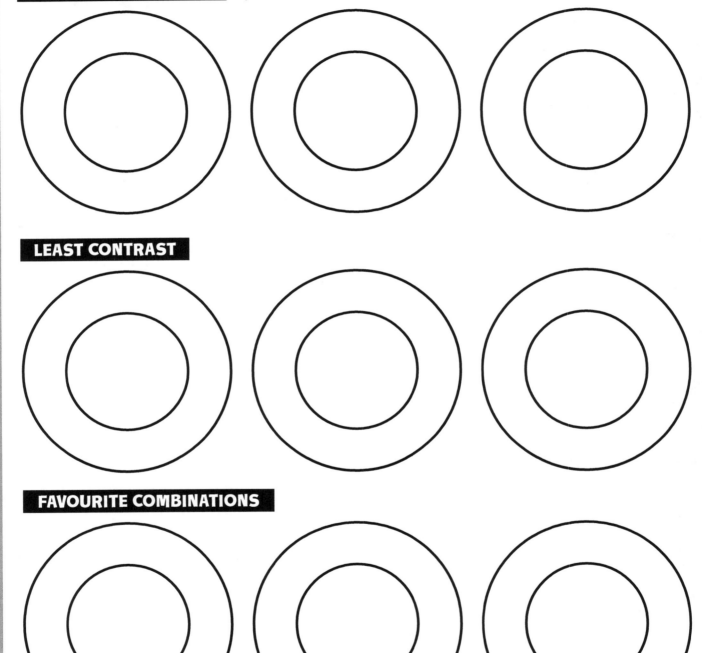

COLOURS AND THEIR MEANINGS

RED — energy, excitement, momentum, strength, power, warmth, love, anger, danger, fire, aggression, passion

YELLOW — joy, happiness, hopefulness, optimism, imagination, sunshine, summer, gold, dishonesty, fear, betrayal, envy, illness

BLUE — harmony, peace, calm, steadiness, unity, trust, confidence, cleanliness, order, security, loyalty, sky, water, cold, technology, sadness

ORANGE — energy, balance, warmth, enthusiasm, expansiveness, glitz, attention-grabbing

GREEN — nature, environment, health, good luck, renewal, youth, vitality, spring, generosity, fertility, jealousy, inexperience, hardship

PURPLE — royalty, spirituality, nobility, mystery, transformation, wisdom, enlightenment, cruelty, arrogance, mourning

GREY — safety, dependability, intelligence, modesty, maturity, depression, boredom, old-fashioned, practical

WHITE — admiration, purity, minimalism, cleanliness, peace, innocence, youth, birth, winter, snow, virtue, hygiene

BROWN — earth, home, outdoors, trustworthiness, comfort, staying power, strength, simplicity, calm

BLACK — power, dominance, formality, elegance, wealth, mystery, terror, evil, anonymity, unhappiness, sadness, remorse, death

7

COLOUR IN ADVERTISING

In advertising, the colours chosen and the way they are used can help to sell a product or convey a message. Look at different advertisements in magazines. Choose one advertisement and explain, using your own ideas and the meanings of different colours, how it uses colour to sell a product or convey a message.

Advertisement: _____

How does the use of colour help to sell the product or convey a message?

_____

_____

_____

_____

_____

_____

_____

_____

_____

_____

_____

_____

_____

COLOUR IN ADVERTISING

Create an advertisement for one of the following:

• vacation	• perfume	• restaurant
• car	• home	• public service announcement
• clothing	• cereal	(e.g., health, safety)

Think about what colour scheme will engage your target audience. What colours should you use to persuade people that they should buy your product or service? If you are creating a public service announcement, what colours will reinforce your message?

What you need:

• Colours and Their Meanings handout
• Paper
• Colouring materials

Plan

What is your advertisement for?

_____

_____

_____

_____

What colours are you going to use and why?

_____

_____

_____

_____

Rough Outline

Colour the picture using only cool colours.

Choose a colour scheme and on a separate piece of paper explain your reasoning.

ELEMENTS OF DESIGN: VALUE

Using tempera paint, create shades of the following colours by adding black, a little bit at a time.

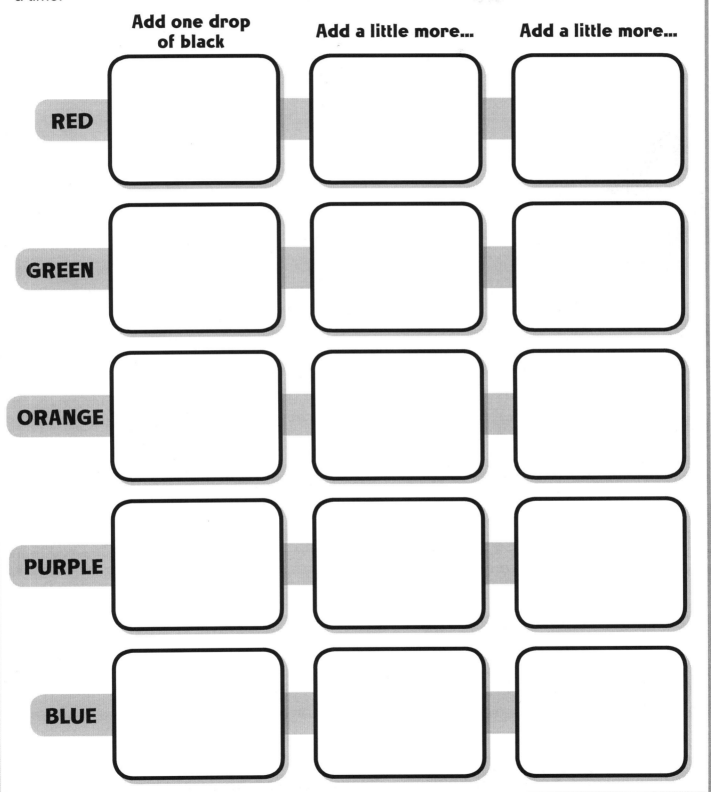

	Add one drop of black	**Add a little more...**	**Add a little more...**
RED			
GREEN			
ORANGE			
PURPLE			
BLUE			

13

ELEMENTS OF DESIGN: VALUE

Using tempera paint, create tints of the following colours by adding white, a little bit at a time.

	Add one drop of white	Add a little more...	Add a little more...
RED			
GREEN			
ORANGE			
PURPLE			
BLUE			

Colour the picture using only tones of black and white.

ELEMENTS OF DESIGN: SHAPE

Activity 1: Shape Picture

What you need:
- Black construction paper
- Scissors
- Coloured construction paper
- Glue

What to do:

1. Ask students to plan and compose a picture based on geometric shapes.
2. Have students cut out various geometric shapes to use for their picture.
3. Once students have planned a detailed composition, have students glue the shapes onto the black construction paper.

Activity 2: Shape Collage

What you need:
- Paper
- Watercolours
- Paintbrushes
- Rulers
- Black markers
- Pencils

What to do:

1. Instruct students to produce a design of black outlines of overlapping geometric shapes. Encourage students to use a variety of shapes in their design.
2. Next, have students paint sections of the design using a specific approach, such as complementary colours only, secondary colours only, different tints, and so on.
3. When students have finished, discuss with them their approach to their artwork.

16

Find and list places where you see or use the following geometric shapes in everyday life.

Circle

Octagon

Triangle

Trapezoid

Square

Hexagon

Rectangle

Oval

ORGANIC SHAPE HUNT

Organic Shape: Non-geometric or free-flowing shape.

Look around and draw different organic shapes you see.

18

A tangram is an ancient Chinese puzzle made from seven geometric shapes.
The objective is to form a specific shape with these seven pieces.

1. Carefully cut out the tangram shapes below.

2. Use the tangram shapes to construct an animal, person or thing. Your new shape design must contain all the pieces, which may not overlap.

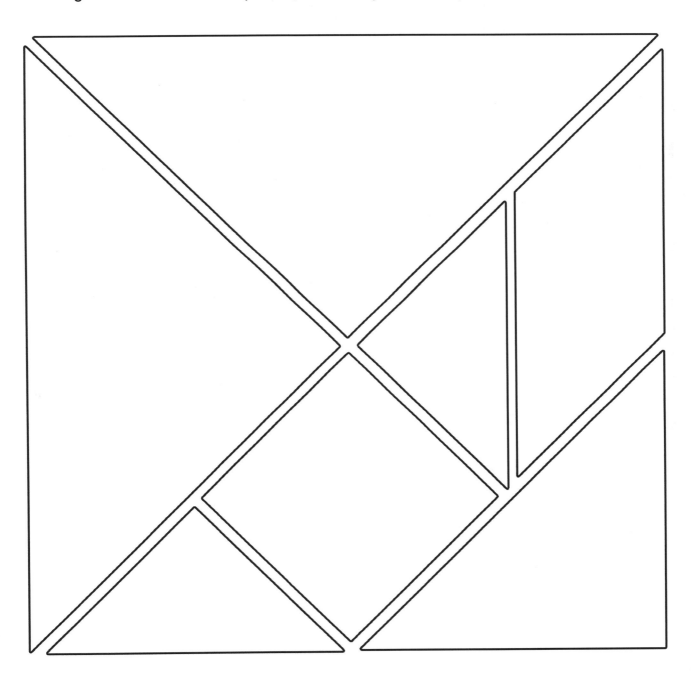

How many of these tangram animal puzzles can you solve?

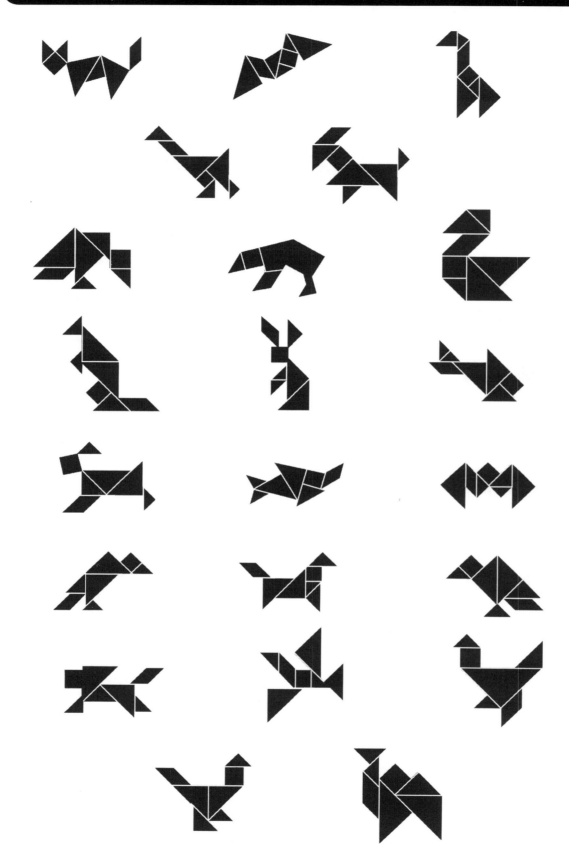

GEOMETRIC DESIGN

Colour the geometric design using different shades of only one colour.

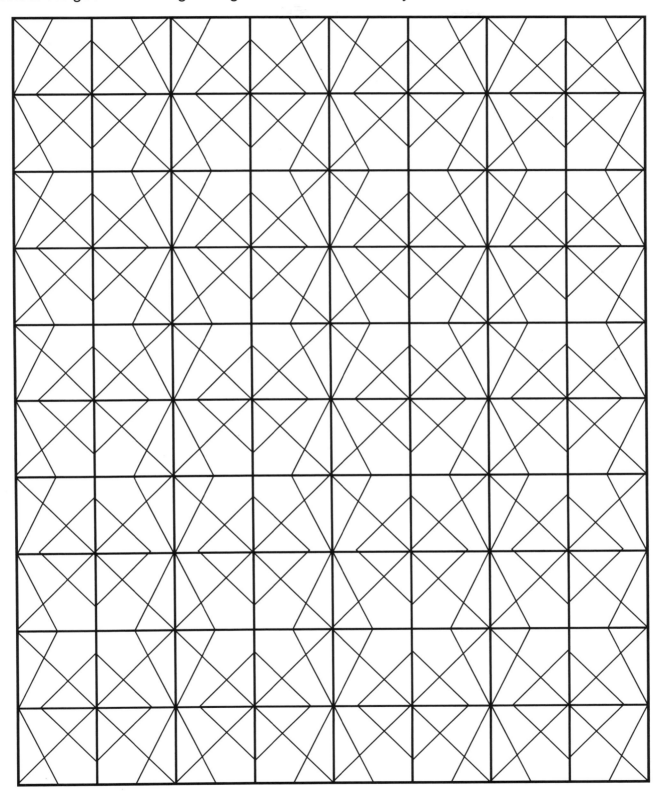

Colour the geometric design using primary colours.

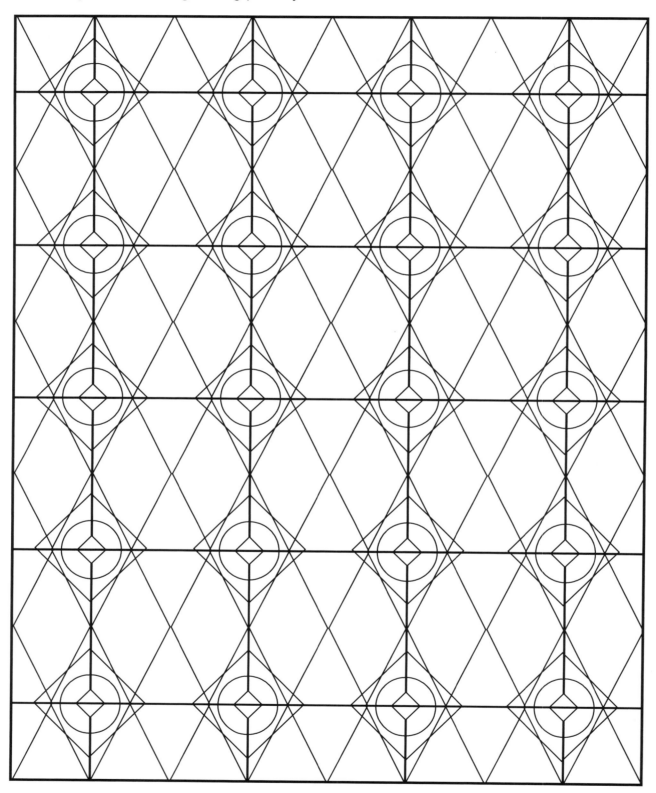

Colour the geometric design using tertiary colours.

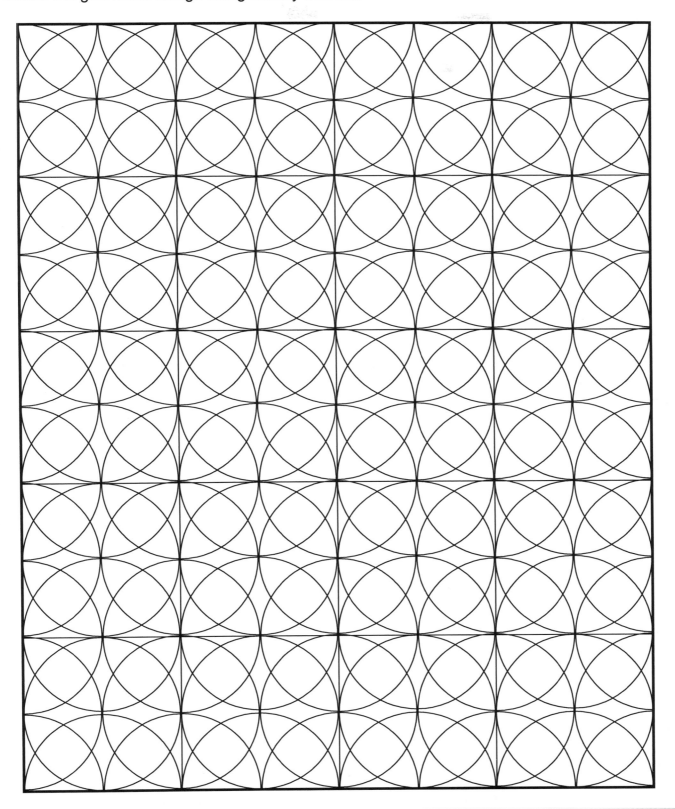

ELEMENTS OF DESIGN: LINE

Activity 1: Outlining Objects

What you need:
- Crayons
- Pastels
- Paint and paintbrushes
- A variety of everyday objects such as scissors, drinking glasses, cans, or toothbrush
- Paper
- Chalk
- Pencil crayons

What to do:
1. Demonstrate for students how to trace the contour of various objects to produce a pleasing line composition.
2. Invite students to trace various objects, overlapping them to produce their own line compositions. Encourage students to use assorted drawing materials and colours and to notice the types of lines created by each.

Activity 2: Contour Drawing

What you need:
- Paper • Small fruits • HB pencil

What to do:
1. Explain to students that they will be completing a contour drawing of a small fruit such as a pear or banana. Review the term contour drawing.
2. Have students begin by placing the fruit of their choice near the paper. Students may find it helpful to strive to make their drawings the same size as the actual fruit.
3. Then encourage students to begin their contour drawing. They should choose a point on the edge of the fruit and follow its contour with their eyes, allowing their hand to copy the shape of the fruit onto the paper.
4. Caution students not to rush. They should try to draw every curve, including strong lines on the fruit such as a fold or crease.
5. Remind students that the purpose of this activity is to practise getting their hand and eye to do the same thing, by judging the size and shape of the edges the student can see.
6. Once done, have students review their drawings and consider whether their drawings match the real-life shapes of the fruit. Discuss whether the proportions are correct and whether enough details were included.
7. Repeat this drawing activity using different everyday objects.

26

ELEMENTS OF DESIGN: LINE

Activity 3: Blind Contour Drawing

What you need:

• Paper • HB pencil

What to do:

1. Explain to students that they will complete a blind contour drawing of their hand. Review the terms contour drawing and blind contour drawing.

2. Have students begin by placing their pencils near the bottom edge of the paper.

3. Then encourage students to begin drawing. They should look at the edge of their wrist and slowly follow the contour of one hand with their eyes, allowing the other hand to slowly and carefully draw the line they see on the paper. Remind students to keep their eyes on the hand they are drawing, not the hand that is moving! Encourage students not to rush and to record every curve and bump they see. If they get to a fold or crease in the skin, they should follow it in and then back out to the side.

4. Have students review their drawings and comment on the accuracy of their drawings. What surprised them about this activity and the results?

5. Repeat the activity using students' running shoes.

Activity 4: Sgraffito

What you need:

• Paper (untextured)
• Crayons
• Paintbrushes
• Thick tempera paint

• Objects that scratch, such as toothpicks, tongue depressors, combs, coins and plastic utensils

What to do:

1. Invite students to draw broad bands of colour, using crayons, on a piece of paper that has a smooth surface. Remind students to apply pressure on the crayons as they draw.

2. Once completed, have students paint over the entire paper with the black tempera paint.

3. After the paint dries encourage students to scratch designs onto the paper using the objects. This technique is called sgraffito.

ELEMENTS OF DESIGN: LINE

Activity 5: Rhythm and Line

What you need:
- Crayons
- Pastels
- Different types of music
- Paper
- Chalk
- Pencil crayons

What to do:

1. Choose and play a piece of music for students and have them trace the rhythm of the music with a finger in the air. Ask them to describe the line their finger creates.

2. Now, have students draw the line that represents the rhythm of the music using the material(s) and colour(s) of their choice. Have students add more such lines above and below the first line.

3. Repeat the activity with different types of music and discuss as a class why students chose the types of lines and colours they did for each.

Activity 6: Experiment with Lines

What you need:
- Assorted colours of tissue paper
- Water
- Shallow pan
- White paper

What to do:

1. Have students moisten pieces of tissue paper by dipping them in a shallow pan of water.

2. Next, lay the wet tissue paper onto white paper in interesting arrangements.

3. Allow the tissue paper to dry.

4. Once the tissue paper has dried, have students outline the interesting shapes or patterns that result.

Draw examples of the following lines.

Thin Lines

Thick Lines

Wavy Lines

Dotted Lines

Zigzag Lines

Fill in the sections of the picture using at least five different types of lines and your own colour scheme.

Colour the picture. **BRAIN STRETCH**: Why do you think the artist used curved lines to represent water?

31

ELEMENTS OF DESIGN: FORM

Activity 1: Sand Sculpture Dough

What you need:

- 4 cups clean sand (not beach sand)
- 2 cups cornstarch
- 2 cups water
- Plastic utensils for carving

What to do:

1. Mix all ingredients in a saucepan.
2. Heat the mixture over medium heat and stir until it becomes as thick as modelling clay.
3. Once the mixture is the right consistency, allow it to cool before handling. **Note:** You may wish to make the dough beforehand and store it in an airtight container.
4. Encourage students to notice the interesting texture of the dough as they mould or "sculpt" it into various forms.
5. Allow the completed forms to air dry.

Activity 2: Papier Mâché Sculpture

What you need:

- Large plastic bowl
- Newsprint
- Hot water
- Plastic bag
- Flour
- Water
- Tempera paint
- Paintbrushes

What to do:

1. First have students tear enough small squares of newsprint to fill a large plastic bowl.
2. Cover the scraps with hot water and soak them overnight.
3. Demonstrate for students how to squeeze out the excess water from the newsprint scraps. Place the scraps into a plastic bag.
4. Make a paste of flour and water. Use 1/3 cup flour for every 1/4 cup water. Combine the paste with the newspaper scraps, using 1 cup of paste for every 3 cups of paper. Knead this papier mâché clay in the plastic bag.
5. When the consistency of the clay is good for moulding, encourage students to form animals, insects, flowers or other small objects.
6. Let the papier mâché sculptures air dry and then paint them.

Chalkboard Publishing © 2012

ELEMENTS OF DESIGN: FORM

Activity 3: Drawing People

What you need:

- White paper • Pencil and eraser • Colouring materials

What to do:

1. Demonstrate for students how the human body may be looked upon as a series of connected oval or sausage-like shapes.

2. Use a student as a model to draw, and help students see the breakdown of the oval body parts.

3. Once you have drawn all of the oval segments of the human form, erase the overlapping lines where body parts connect. Point out to students that there are joints where many body parts connect. Joints include the shoulders, knees and wrists.

4. Next, add clothing and other features to complete the drawing. Show students how to add lines to the area around joints to show bent limbs and creases.

5. Students are now ready to draw their humans. Have students work in pairs, so that they can be models for each other. Encourage students to draw their partner in various positions.

Activity 4: Animated People

What you need:

- White paper • Pencil and eraser • Colouring materials

What to do:

1. Review with students how the human body may be looked upon as a series of connected oval or sausage-like shapes.

2. Next, have students work in pairs. One partner will pose while the other partner will draw the partner in a series of 3–5 positions that show action, such as when participating in a sport.

3. Encourage students to draw details on their animated person and facial expressions.

4. Students should also add a background to their picture.

SYMMETRICAL DRAWINGS

Draw the other half of the picture using the grid as a guide. Colour the picture.

SYMMETRICAL DRAWINGS

Draw the other half of the picture using the grid as a guide. Colour the picture.

Draw the other half of the picture using the grid as a guide. Colour the picture.

Cut out a face from a magazine. Cut it in half and glue one half below. Draw and colour the other half of the face.

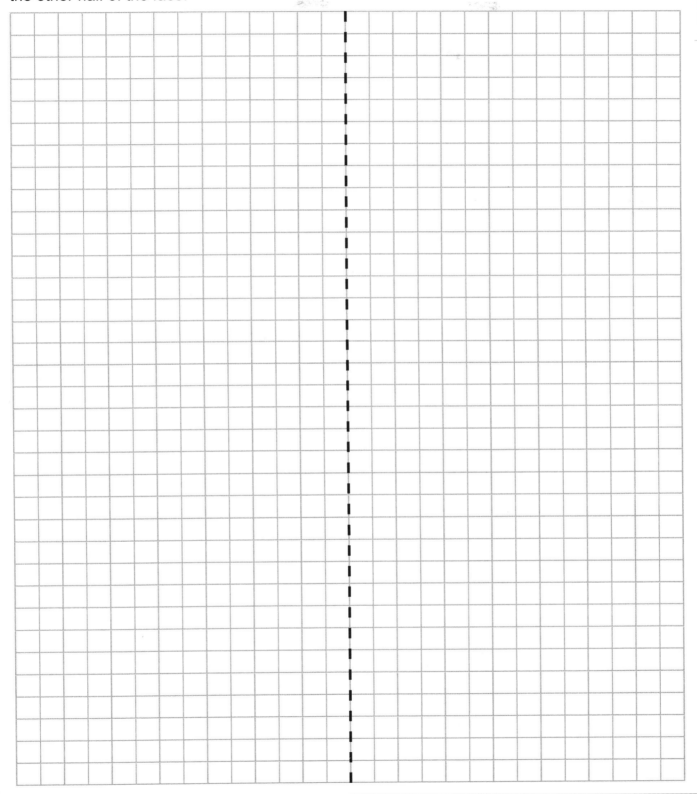

Allegory: The use of symbolic figures to represent abstract ideas such as honour and sacrifice.

Design a Canadian war memorial. Think about the symbols that you would like to incorporate into your design and explain your thinking on a separate piece of paper.

Use these body parts to draw your own fantasy creature.

Use these body parts to draw your own fantasy creature.

FANTASY CREATURE FILL-IN

Use these body parts to draw your own fantasy creature.

ELEMENTS OF DESIGN: TEXTURE

Activity 1: Sandpaper Designs

What you need:
- Sandpaper • Crayons • Iron • Paper

What to do:

1. Invite students to colour a design or picture on sandpaper. They should press heavily into the paper as they colour, to deposit a lot of wax onto the sandpaper.

2. Next, demonstrate for students how to carefully lay paper on top of their picture and run a warm iron over the paper. Show students how the heat will transfer a gravel-like print of their picture onto the paper.

3. After students have made one print, they can colour their design or picture using a different colour scheme and make a second print

Activity 2: Texture Mania

What you need:
- Large piece of paper
- Glue
- Black markers
- Paint

- Various materials such as sawdust, torn construction paper, tissue paper, crushed eggshells, newsprint, etc.

- Paintbrushes

What to do:

1. Instruct students to draw an outline picture on their paper using a black marker.

2. Then, have students glue on different materials to fill in the different sections of the drawing.

3. Once the materials have dried and all of the sections of the drawing have been filled, encourage students to add paint to their artwork.

43

EXPERIMENT WITH TEXTURE

Encourage students to create different textures with the tools, materials, and papers listed below. They can use the textures to create a collage or to fill sections of a picture.

Out-of-the-Ordinary Painting Tools

- Fingers
- Sticks
- Blocks of wood
- Branches
- Rope
- Feathers
- Leaves
- Sponges
- Tissues
- Brushes
- Cotton swabs
- Cotton balls
- Plastic pot scrubbers
- Plastic wrap
- Makeup brushes

Excellent Drawing and Painting Materials

- Crayons
- Pencils
- Pastels
- Chalk
- Charcoal
- Ink pen
- Water-based markers
- Acrylic paint
- Makeup
- Tempera paint
- Felt tip pens
- Pencil crayons
- Watercolours
- Food colouring

A Variety of Surfaces on Which to Paint or Draw

- Newsprint
- Paper plates
- Blocks of wood
- Tissue paper
- Paper bags
- Sandpaper
- Wet paper
- Cardboard
- Fabric
- Plastic wrap
- Paper towels
- Waxed paper
- Aluminum foil
- Stones
- Foam

CREATE DIFFERENT TEXTURES

Corn Syrup Paint

Make a striking paint with an interesting texture by combining food colouring and light corn syrup. Mix up as many colours as needed. Encourage students to paint different landscapes or oceanscapes. Students may wish to first create an outline drawing with a permanent marker before painting. Be sure to allow more than a day of drying time.

Flour-and-Water Fingerpaint

This paint will help you to achieve great textures when fingerpainting. Mix 1 cup flour, 1 cup water and 2 teaspoons salt in a small container to make a paint with the consistency of thick gravy. Add in the desired food colouring. Repeat the process for as many colours as needed.

Glossy Paint

Give tempera paint a wet, glossy look by combining 1 part white glue and 1 part tempera paint.

Puff Paint

Have students create unique pictures using puff paint. Combine 1 cup salt, 1 cup sugar and the desired food colouring in a squeeze bottle. Shake the ingredients and squeeze the paint out of the bottle onto the paper.

Sand Paint

Sand paint offers an interesting option when striving to create texture in a picture. Begin by having students create a simple outline drawing. Then make the sand paint by combining 1 part sand and 5 parts powdered tempera. Encourage students to experiment when mixing the sand and tempera to achieve the desired colour. Next, when a few sand paint colours have been made, use a wooden craft stick to spread a thin layer of glue in one section of the outline drawing. Then, using a spoon, gently pour the sand paint into the glue-covered section. Lightly lift the paper to shake off any excess sand paint. Allow the sand painting to dry, and seal it using hairspray.

Wax Resist

As wax and water don't mix, the wax resist technique can be used to mask out areas to preserve the white of the paper or the colour beneath and to create appealing textures. Draw or colour with a wax crayon and then wash over it with a water-based paint.

MAKING TEXTURED PAPER

What you need:

- Large tub
- Assorted papers
- Cornstarch
- Books
- Blender

- Wax paper
- Rolling pin
- Warm water
- Measuring spoons

- Materials that add colour and texture (e.g., glitter, food colouring, seeds)
- Materials with which to imprint the paper (e.g., plants, lace, buttons)

What to do:

1. Tear the assorted papers into tiny bits and pieces. Students can separate the papers by colour.

2. Soak the torn paper in a tub of warm water for at least a few hours.

3. Add torn paper and water to a blender. Use 1 cup paper for every 2–3 cups water. Blend the mixture on medium-high until it is creamy and smooth, to make a pulp.

4. Add 1 tablespoon of cornstarch, to make the resulting paper less porous to ink and paper. Students can also add food colouring, glitter, or tiny materials that will create texture in their papers (e.g., seeds). Blend the mixture for about 10 seconds after each addition.

5. Lay a large piece of wax paper on a table.

6. Measure out about half a cup of pulp and squeeze out excess water by hand. Smooth the pulp out onto the wax paper in a thin layer.

7. Students can press plants, lace, or other textured materials into the pulp, to create imprints.

8. Lay a second piece of wax paper over the thin layer of pulp and use a rolling pin to roll out any excess water.

9. Repeat the above process to make layers of new and different papers.

10. Weigh down all the new papers with books and allow them to dry.

11. When the papers are dry, carefully peel away the layers of wax paper.

Find examples of different textures and reproduce them by making rubbings on this page.

Lay the landscape on different surfaces (such as sandpaper) while you colour it. This will produce a variety of textures.

Paint the landscape using watercolours.

Fill in sections of the landscape using different colours of Plasticine.

Colour the landscape using oil pastels and set it with hairspray.

Fill in the sections of the picture using torn bits of construction paper.

ELEMENTS OF DESIGN: SPACE

Activity 1: Landscape

What you need:

• White paper   • Oil pastels   • Cotton balls for smudging

What to do:

1. Review with students the art terms foreground, middle ground and background and tell students that they will be painting a landscape. Look at and discuss examples of landscapes.

2. To begin, show students how to lightly sketch with their pencil these three sections using ground, water and ground.

3. Instruct students to fill each section with paint. Encourage students to mix colours and to use more than one shade or tint of colour.

4. Once the sections are completely covered with paint, have students add details and objects to the sections using darker colours. Remind students that objects in the foreground are the most prominent and appear to be the closest to the viewer. Alternatively, objects that are smaller are intended to appear farther away from the viewer.

Activity 2: Streetscape in One-Point Perspective

What you need:

• Colouring materials   • Pencil   • Eraser   • Ruler

What to do:

1. Review with students the art terms perspective, horizon line and vanishing point. Show examples of each term and how they are used in artwork.

2. Explain to students that they will draw a streetscape in one-point perspective. Have students begin by drawing a horizon line on their papers.

3. Next, students should find the midpoint of the horizon line and mark it as the vanishing point for their drawing.

4. Demonstrate for students how to mark the bottom right and left corners of their paper and then draw a line from each mark to the vanishing point. This will create the illusion of a street.

5. Have students add three-dimensional buildings along each side of the street. Remind students that buildings should decrease in size as they approach the vanishing point.

6. Encourage students to add other details to their drawings, along both the street and the horizon line.

ELEMENTS OF DESIGN: SPACE

Activity 3: Light, Shade and Shadow

What you need:

- Black construction paper
- White construction paper
- Bristol board
- Pencil
- Eraser
- Glue
- Masking tape

What to do:

1. Tape a large piece of white construction paper onto a wall in a room with dim lighting.

2. One student holds the flashlight so that it shines onto the white construction paper. Another student sits between the light and the paper so that the shadow of their profile appears on the paper. A third student traces the outline of the second student's profile onto the paper.

3. Repeat steps 1 and 2 until each student has a copy of their profile.

4. Instruct students to cut their profile out of the white paper, place it onto three pieces of black construction paper, trace around it, and cut out the resulting three black silhouettes.

5. Students glue the black silhouettes onto white construction paper to create a series of shadows.

Activity 4: Positive and Negative Shapes

What you need:

- Squares of construction paper (black and coloured)
- Scissors
- Glue

What to do:

1. Discuss with students the concept of positive and negative spaces in artwork.

2. Instruct students to trace one or more geometric shapes onto one square of black construction paper and one square of coloured construction paper.

3. Have students cut out the geometric shapes.

4. Next, have students glue the black geometric shapes onto coloured construction paper and the coloured geometric shapes onto black construction paper.

THINKING ABOUT SPACE

Colour the picture. **BRAIN STRETCH:** How is the element of space used in this picture?

55

Chalkboard Publishing © 2012

Complete the picture by adding a horizon line and vanishing point. Add details to the picture and colour.

Complete the picture using different elements of design. On a separate piece of paper, explain how you used the elements.

Complete the picture using different elements of design. On a separate piece of paper, explain how you used the elements.

CUTOUT ART

Create a picture using images cut out of old magazines.

WORKING WITH ELEMENTS OF DESIGN

Add a logo to the hockey player's uniform. Think about elements of design and add other details to the picture. Explain what you did on a separate piece of paper.

Use elements of design to colour the picture. Explain what you did on a separate piece of paper.

ART DISCUSSION PROMPTS: LOOKING AT A PAINTING

Description

- Describe the subject of the painting.
- What colours do you see?
- What shapes do you see?
- What textures do you see?
- What kind of lines do you see?
- What kind of objects do you see?
- What kind of forms do you see?

Analysis

- What is the focal point of the painting?
- Is there an element of design that is most prominent in the painting? Explain.
- Do you think the composition is balanced? Explain.
- Does the artist show movement in the painting? If so, how?
- Does the painting have a sense of three dimensions?
- What angle of view do you think the artist had when painting this subject? Explain your thinking.

Interpretation

- What kind of mood do you think the artist is trying to encourage when viewing the painting?
- How does the painting make you feel?
- What message or meaning do you think the artist is trying to convey?
- Why do you think the artist chose to paint this particular subject?

Personal Opinion

- Do you like the painting? Why or why not?
- What, if anything, does this painting remind you of? Explain.
- The painting is a good example of … or The painting is a bad example of …
- Do you think the title of the painting is a good one? Explain.
- Would you like to see more paintings from this artist? Why or why not?
- Would you buy this painting? Why or why not?

62

ARTIST-INSPIRED ART IDEAS

Artist: Theodore Dragonieri

Theodore Dragonieri is a Canadian artist who fixes old shoes, then paints and collages them in the styles of famous artists.

What you need:

- Pictures of Theodore Dragonieri's painted shoes
- Pairs of old shoes
- Paintbrushes
- Acrylic or tempera paints with white glue added to them
- Paper and pencils
- Water and containers

What to do:

1. Display pictures of Theodore Dragonieri's shoe art and discuss it as a class. Ask students what they think of it.
2. Ask students to think about artists they like. Have them choose one of the artists.
3. Have students sketch a drawing that they will paint onto the shoes.
4. Distribute materials and have students remove any laces from the shoes.
5. When students have finalized their design, have them paint it onto the shoes. To make dark shoes easier to paint on, students may first prime them with white paint.
6. When the shoes are finished, have classmates try to guess which artist each student was inspired by.

Artist: Robert Bateman

Robert Bateman was born May 24, 1930, in Toronto, Ontario. He is famous for realistic drawings of wildlife. See examples of his art at www.robertbateman.ca.

What you need:

- Wildlife photographs (calendars are usually an excellent source)
- Colouring pencils
- Paper

What to do:

1. Show and discuss examples of Robert Bateman's art. What do students think of it?
2. Have students choose a wildlife photograph as a reference for their realistic drawing.
3. Next, share with students tips on realistic drawing. They should start with a simple pencil sketch and then add details. Encourage students to take their time and think about shading, line and colours.
4. Students should share and discuss their completed drawings with the class.

ARTIST-INSPIRED ART IDEAS

Artist: Norval Morrisseau

Norval Morriseau was a famous Canadian Ojibwa artist known for his unique style, called the Eastern Woodland Style. This style can also be seen in the works of Daphne Odjig, Carl Ray and Blake Debassige. See examples of his work at http://coghlanart.com/norval1.htm.

What you need:

- Large pieces of heavy white paper for each student
- Paintbrushes
- Tempera paint with glue added to make the consistency thick
- Images of animals for reference

What to do:

1. Show and discuss examples of Norval Morrisseau's art. What do students think of it? In Morrisseau's unique style (which is reminiscent of an X-ray), the viewer sees the person or animal painted, as well as the energy within that person or animal.
2. Next, ask students to choose a subject for their painting, such as a fish, a bird or a turtle.
3. Then, have students sketch the outline of their subject on their paper.
4. Once done, discuss with students how they think they should represent the energy and emotion inside of their subject. Make a list of ideas for all students.
5. Encourage students to use different elements of design, such as line, colour and shape, inside the subject of their painting.
6. Lastly, have students share their choices for their artwork.

Artist: David Ruben Piqtoukun

David Ruben Piqtoukun is an internationally renowned Inuit artist born in Paulatuk, Northwest Territories. He is the sculptor who crafted an inukshuk for the grounds of the McMichael Canadian Art Collection. An inukshuk is a stone marker that sometimes resembles a human. It can serve as a marker, a navigational aid or a message centre. Inukshuks still stand in many areas of the Arctic, some dating before 1000 BC.
See examples of David Ruben Piqtoukun work at http://www.jacobgallery.com/art_gallery/inuit_art/David_Ruben_Piqtoukun/original-eskimo-sculptures.html.

What you need:

- White paper • Grey construction paper • Glue

What to do:

1. Have students look at examples of inukshuks.
2. Then have students tear and glue grey construction paper to construct their own inukshuk on their paper. Encourage students to write about their inukshuk and what it stands for.

ARTIST-INSPIRED ART IDEAS

Artists: Group Of Seven

The Group of Seven was a group of famous Canadian landscape painters in the 1920s, first consisting of Franklin Carmichael, Lawren Harris, A. Y. Jackson, Franz Johnston, A. J. Casson, Arthur Lismer, J. E. H. MacDonald and Frederick Varley. Tom Thomson (who died in 1917) and Emily Carr were closely associated with the Group of Seven but were never official members. These painters were inspired by the distinctive character of the different Canadian landscapes. Together, they developed a unique style to represent the various rugged regions of Canada. Examples of their work can be seen at http://www.mcmichael.com.

Activity 1: Looking at the Paintings of the Group of Seven

Invite students to examine various paintings completed by members of the Group of Seven. Then, as a class, choose a specific painting to look at more closely and to discuss. Use the blackline master Art Discussion Prompts: Looking at a Painting as a springboard for discussion. Next, have students work with a partner to review a different painting using the blackline master.

Activity 2: Similarities and Differences

Have students work independently or with a partner to examine two paintings by members of the Group of Seven. Students will then complete the blackline master Similarities and Differences. When they are ready, ask students to share their findings during a class discussion.

Activity 3: Art Appreciation: Portrait of A Famous Artist

Have students study a member of the Group of Seven and create a brochure celebrating the painter's life and work. Students should complete a timeline that includes all of the important events in the painter's life using the black line master An Artist's Life. Other topics to include in the brochure include Artist Style, Artist Inspiration and Examples of the Artist's Work.

Activity 4: Group of Seven Art Unit

There is a wonderful Group of Seven art unit available online from the National Gallery of Canada at http://cybermuse.gallery.ca/cybermuse/teachers/plans/intro_e.jsp?lessonid=2. The unit includes background information, hands-on activities and a glossary.

AN ARTIST'S LIFE

Create a timeline of the significant events in the life a famous artist. Use this graphic organizer to help you.

Name of artist: _____

I chose this famous artist because _____

_____

DATE	EVENT

SIMILARITIES AND DIFFERENCES

Describe two artworks.

Artist and description of artwork

Artist and description of artwork

Compare

How are the artworks **similar**?

Contrast

How are the artworks **different**?

DIRECT DRAW

Encourage students to think of art as the personal interpretation of ideas. This quick activity demonstrates how students given the same directions will each produce a unique artwork. Collect and display all of the students' completed artworks. You will have a wonderful collection of abstract art based on shape, colour and line.

WHAT YOU NEED:

• Square piece of paper
• Colouring materials

WHAT TO DO:

1. Tell students that they will each complete a piece of art by following your oral directions. Before you begin, ask students to predict whether or not all the students' works will look the same.

2. Give each student the same materials.

3. Call out directions. For example:

   • Draw a thin line across the page.

   • Draw a thick line across the page.

   • Draw a circle anywhere on the page.

   • Draw a triangle somewhere on the page.

   • ...

   Add directions of your choice that will reinforce art vocabulary. Give students enough time to follow each direction before calling out the next one.

4. When all the directions have been called out, have students compare and contrast their artworks with a partner. How are the pieces the same? How are they different?

5. Display the students' artworks.

SKETCHBOOK DRAWING IDEAS

Portrait

- Draw a self-portrait. Look at yourself in a mirror for reference.
- Draw a self-portrait of yourself 50 years from now.
- Draw a portrait of a friend or family member. Think about how you can show something about their personality in the portrait.
- Re-create a black and white photograph. Think about the tones in the photograph and how to imitate them.
- Practise drawing different eyes, lips, noses, ears and types of hair. Look through magazines and other materials to find a variety of sizes, shapes and poses.
- Draw a series of portraits of a family member using photographs taken at different stages of their life. For example: baby, child, teenager, adult and senior. Think about what physical characteristics remain constant.
- Practise drawing different parts of the body in various positions. Ask a friend or family member to model arms, legs, heads and shoulders.
- Draw a series of hands in a variety of positions or overlapping them.

Design

- Design a CD cover for your favourite group or singer.
- Design a magazine cover for your favourite magazine.
- Design a logo for your school or a school team.
- Design an advertisement for a vacation destination.
- Design a new cover for a book.
- Design a tattoo for a specific person.
- Design the can for a new drink.
- Design the outside of your dream house.
- Design your ultimate bedroom.
- Design a new Canadian stamp.
- Design a new Canadian coin.
- Design a new outfit.
- Design a car.
- Design a new Canadian flag.
- Design a cityscape from the future.

Still Life

- Draw an attractive flower arrangement.
- Draw a plant in great detail.
- Draw a piece of furniture with attention to colour, shading and texture.
- Draw a stuffed animal.
- Draw a favourite toy.
- Draw a bowl of fruit.
- Draw an arrangement of three-dimensional figures with attention to shading.

Chalkboard Publishing © 2012

SEASONAL ART IDEAS

FALL

- Paint a fall mural on the classroom windows using a mixture of equal parts dishwashing liquid and paint (use washable liquid paint or powdered tempera paint). Encourage students to add as many details as possible.

- Sketch a still life of a cornucopia, or arrange and sketch a still life of items that represent fall (e.g., fall leaves, corn).

- Make leaf rubbings using chalk and set them with hairspray. Encourage students to arrange and overlap different types of leaves in their rubbings.

- Use black charcoal to draw spooky Halloween pictures.

- Produce beautiful "stained glass" Christmas windows using black construction paper and tissue paper. Students cut out Christmas symbols from the black construction paper, leaving the "window frame." Then students carefully paste different colours of tissue paper to create a stained glass effect.

WINTER

- Paint a winter mural on the classroom windows using a mixture of equal parts dishwashing liquid and paint (use washable liquid paint or powdered tempera paint).

- Draw a winter scene using crayons and apply a wash with salt added, for a snowy effect.

- Draw people in motion participating in various winter sports and activities.

- Make Valentine's Day pendants using self-hardening clay. Students can mould their own shape or use cookie cutters as guides. Paint the pendants with acrylic paint once the clay is dry.

- Go outside on a snowy day and create snow sculptures!

SEASONAL ART IDEAS

SPRING

- Paint a spring mural on the classroom windows using a mixture of equal parts dishwashing liquid and paint (use washable liquid paint or powdered tempera paint).

- Create mosaics using seeds.

- Use papier mâché to decorate old vases in spring colours. Ask students to bring old vases from home.

- Draw and colour realistic pictures of spring flowers. Students should use close-up photographs of flowers as references.

- Draw a still life of an Easter lily arrangement

- Design an Earth Day poster.

- Decorate paper Easter eggs. Students cut egg shapes out of construction paper and draw line patterns on them with water-based markers. Students can trace over the marker lines with white glue to produce an embossed effect (the glue will dry clear).

- Produce beautiful insect and flower "stained glass" windows using black construction paper and tissue paper. Students cut out the desired shapes from the black construction paper, leaving the "window frame." Then students carefully paste different colours of tissue paper to create a stained glass effect.

SUMMER

- Paint a summer mural on the classroom windows using a mixture of equal parts dishwashing liquid and paint (use washable liquid paint or powdered tempera paint).

- Make miniature kites. Use straws or wooden craft sticks to construct the frame and cover it with tissue paper. Attach string.

- Draw the outline of a summer scene and fill sections of the drawing using mixed media.

- Draw a still life of beach toys.

- Use oil pastels to draw a still life of a bowl of fruit.

- Build a sandcastle using sand clay. Once the sandcastle is finished, students should gently pat dry sand on the moist clay.

ART RUBRICS

UNDERSTANDING OF ART CONCEPTS RUBRIC

LEVEL	DESCRIPTORS
4	Student shows a thorough understanding of all or almost all concepts and consistently gives appropriate and complete explanations independently. No teacher support is needed.
3	Student shows a good understanding of most concepts and usually gives complete or nearly complete explanations. Infrequent teacher support is needed.
2	Student shows a satisfactory understanding of most concepts and sometimes gives appropriate, but incomplete, explanations. Teacher support is sometimes needed.
1	Student shows little understanding of concepts and rarely gives complete explanations. Intensive teacher support is needed.

COMMUNICATION OF CONCEPTS RUBRIC

LEVEL	DESCRIPTORS
4	Student almost always uses correct art terminology with clarity and precision during class discussions.
3	Student frequently uses correct art terminology during class discussions.
2	Student occasionally uses correct art terminology during class discussions.
1	Student rarely uses correct art terminology during class discussions.

ANALYSIS OF ARTWORKS RUBRIC

LEVEL	DESCRIPTORS
4	Student accurately describes several dominant elements or principles used by the artist. Student accurately describes how they are used by the artist to reinforce the theme, meaning, mood or feeling of the artwork.
3	Student describes without assistance most of the dominant elements and principles used by the artist. Student describes without assistance how these relate to the meaning, mood, theme or feeling of the artwork.
2	Student describes with little assistance some dominant elements and principles used by the artist. Student needs some teacher prompts to describe how these relate to the meaning, mood, theme or feeling of the artwork.
1	Student has difficulty describing the dominant elements and principles used by the artist in the artwork without direct teacher prompts.

INTERPRETATION OF ARTWORKS RUBRIC

LEVEL	DESCRIPTORS
4	Student analyzes and interprets the meaning of the artwork independently using extensive evidence from the artwork.
3	Student analyzes and interprets the meaning of the artwork with occasional teacher prompts using satisfactory evidence from the artwork.
2	Student requires some teacher prompts to analyze and interpret the meaning of the artwork.
1	Student requires direct teacher assistance to analyze and interpret the meaning of the artwork.

ART RUBRICS

CREATIVE WORK RUBRIC

LEVEL	DESCRIPTORS
4	Student applies almost all of the skills, techniques and art concepts taught.
3	Student applies most of the skills, techniques and art concepts taught.
2	Student applies more than half of the skills, techniques and art concepts taught.
1	Student applies fewer than half of the skills, techniques and art concepts taught.

PARTICIPATION RUBRIC

LEVEL	DESCRIPTORS
4	Student consistently contributes to class discussions and activities by offering ideas and asking questions.
3	Student usually contributes to class discussions and activities by offering ideas and asking questions.
2	Student sometimes contributes to class discussions and activities by offering ideas and asking questions.
1	Student rarely contributes to class discussions and activities by offering ideas and asking questions.

CLASS EVALUATION LIST

Student Name	Class Participation	Understanding of Concepts	Communication of Concepts	Analysis of Artworks	Interpretation of Artworks	Creative Work	Overall Evaluation

ART WEBSITES FOR STUDENTS

A. Pintura: Art Detective
http://www.eduweb.com/pintura

This is a great website that encourages students to become detectives and identify the artist of a mystery painting. By completing the activities students are taught the art concepts of composition, style and subject.

Color Matters
http://www.colormatters.com

Student artists can see how colour affects a person's mind and body, how it is used in design and art, plus lots more. This site explains additive and subtractive colour systems, how the eye sees colours, as well as how other cultures view and use colours.

McMichael Canadian Art Collection

http://www.mcmichael.com

This important Canadian gallery houses a permanent collection of almost 6000 artworks by Tom Thomson, the Group of Seven and their contemporaries, as well as First Nations, Inuit and other artists who have made a contribution to Canada's artistic heritage. Teachers and students can view and research objects in the collection online.

Artists in Canada

http://www.artistsincanada.com

A comprehensive national directory of Canadian artists, art galleries and art resources.

The National Gallery of Canada
http://www.gallery.ca

Click on "Learn" to view online exhibitions and to access special interactive features for kids and teens. Themed lesson plans are also available in this part of the website. Each lesson plan includes activities for students at different grade levels.

Origami Fun
http://www.origami-fun.com/printable-origami.html

Students will love experimenting with origami using easy-to-follow printable instructions. Origami projects listed include various flowers, dragon head, talking horse, owl, puffy bunny and much more.

ART GLOSSARY

Abstract art: Art that uses lines, shapes, colours and textures to portray a realistic object in a non-realistic, imaginary way.

Allegory: The use of symbolic figures to represent abstract ideas such as honour and sacrifice.

Analogous colours: Two or more colours that are next to each other on the colour wheel. For example: red, red-orange and orange.

Background: The part of the picture plane that seems to be farthest from the viewer.

Balance: A principle of design that deals with arranging the visual elements in a work of art for harmony of design and proportion.

Cast shadow: The shadow created on a surface when an objects blocks the light.

Complementary colours: Colours opposite each other on the colour wheel. For example: yellow and purple.

Collage: Creating a picture by gluing pieces of materials such as paper, photos, magazine clippings or found objects to a flat surface.

Colour: Colour is an element of design. Eyes see colour when light bounces off an object. The four characteristics of colour are hue, saturation, value and temperature.

Colour wheel: A tool for creating and organizing colours and representing relationships among colours.

Comic: A graphic art form in which images and words are used to tell a story. The images are the main focus and are usually presented in strip or page layout.

Composition: Describes the organization of the elements of design used in an artwork.

Contemporary art: Art created by living artists.

Contour drawing: An outline drawing that characterizes the edge of a form. In "blind" contour drawing, an artist slowly draws each curve on the edges of an object without looking at the paper.

Contour lines: Lines that define the edges, ridges or outline of a shape or form.

Contrast: A principle of design where light colours are used next to dark colours.

ART GLOSSARY

Cool colours: These are the colours that seem to retreat into the background or distance such as green, blue and purple. Colours often associated with cool places, things or feelings.

Elements of design: Colour, line, texture, shape and form.

Focal point: The area in an artwork that attracts the viewer's eye as the centre of interest.

Foreground: The part of the picture plane which appears closest to the viewer and in front of other objects. The foreground is often at the bottom of a picture.

Form: An element of design describing a three-dimensional object.

Foreshortening: A technique used in perspective to produce the illusion of an object retreating into the background.

Horizon line: A level line where water or land seems to end and the sky begins.

Hue: Another word for colour.

Line: An element of design that is used to define shape, contours and outlines. Different lines can suggest a variety of ideas, movements and moods.

Logo: A visual symbol that identifies a business, club, individual or group.

Middle ground: The part of a picture that seems to be in the middle of the picture plane.

Mixed media: Any artwork which uses more than one medium.

Monochromatic: Made using different shades and tints of one colour.

Organic shape: Non-geometric or free-flowing shape.

Perspective: The technique used to represent a three-dimensional world (what we see) on a two-dimensional surface (a piece of paper or canvas) in a way that looks realistic. Perspective is used to generate an illusion of space and depth on a flat surface

Pattern: Lines, colours or shapes repeated in a planned way.

Pointillism: A technique of painting, commonly attributed to Georges Seurat, in which tiny dots of colour are placed close together. From a distance, the dots seem to disappear and the colours blend.

Primary colours: The basic colours—red, blue and yellow—from which all other colours can be mixed.

Secondary colours: The colours produced by mixing equal amounts of any two primary colours: blue and red produce purple, yellow and red make orange, and blue and yellow make green.

Sgraffito: A technique created by scratching into paint to reveal the colours underneath.

Shade: Dark value of a colour made by adding black.

Shape: An element of design describing the outer form or outline of an image created using line, value, colour and/or texture. Shapes may be geometric or organic, positive or negative.

Sketch: A quick drawing that is used as a reference or plan for an artwork.

Space: An element of design that describes the area around, within or between images or other elements of design.

Still life: An artwork depicting a grouping of inanimate objects.

Subject: A topic or idea represented in an artwork.

Symmetry: Symmetry is demonstrated when portions of the object on opposite sides of a line of symmetry are mirror images one of the other.

Tertiary colours: Colours produced by mixing primary colours with secondary colours.

Tint: Light value of a colour made by adding white.

Texture: An element of design describing the surface quality of an object.

Wash: Created by adding water to paint, making it thin enough to allow colours applied underneath to show through.

Warm colours: Warm colours are used to make an object seem to advance into the foreground. Red, yellow and orange are warm colours. They suggest warm places, things and feelings.

Value: The lightness or darkness of a colour.

Vanishing point: In linear perspective, a position on the horizon where lines or rays between near and distant places appear to come together.

ARTIST extraordinaire!

Keep up the terrific art!

FANTASTIC ART!

Keep up the great work!